MW01227858

Frankie and Blossom:

A Honkin' Great Love Story

by

K.S. Wuertz

Mimosa Lake Press

2024

Always to God:
"Let all that you do, be done in love."
1 Corinthians 16:14 NRSA

In Honor of:
My Hometown Heros, and all My Beloveds with Paws!

For:
Callen James & Vivia Ray

A Portion of the proceeds from this book go to help animals who are currently living at Riverside Cemetery and in animal shelters. Remember, so many shelter animals are just waiting for you to come and bring them home!

AND, in thanks, for all the good works of the loving staff at Riverside Cemetery as they watch over Frankie, Blossom and all the winged (and four-pawed) residents who call Riverside home.

Dear Reader:

In the Celtic tradition, the interpretation of the bird representing the Holy Spirit was not a dove, but a goose. Why? The goose was seen as a wild spirit which is passionate, noisy, and courageous.

I didn't go looking to write this story, it found me. The past few years have been rough for my hometown - Marshalltown, Iowa. A destructive tornado went through downtown. Then, a devastating derecho almost destroyed Riverside Cemetery, a beautiful, historical landmark in town. What would be next? Then I listened to Steve Hartman's story on the CBS Evening News about a Marshalltown love story. I was inspired!

Frankie and Blossom's story is love in action. Everyone involved was motivated by kindness, selfless giving, and love. This story played out in true Iowa fashion, with little fanfare and no expectations of the resulting wonders. No one expected this story to become front-page news, or for books to be written about Frankie and Blossom. Each person only saw a need, and two grieving creatures who needed to be comforted.

Consequently, they have given us all a great gift! I can't look at pictures of Frankie and Blossom (and all the other creatures who call Riverside home), without smiling. I hope, and know, we humans can cherish and respect all of the other living beings who share our planet. I take great joy in knowing Frankie, Blossom, the ducks, and swans, are so lovingly cared for as they quietly abide amongst the graves, grasses, statues and trees at Riverside.

A special thanks to everyone who shared Frankie and Blossom's joyful romance with us. Thanks to Deb Elliott, my friend, fellow Marshalltown High School graduate (Class of '75), and co-author on this project. For you, the reader, I thank you for buying this book. As with the other books in my 'Souls and Paws' series, the net proceeds will go toward animal welfare. In this case, the proceeds will help care for Frankie, Blossom, the other geese, swans, ducks, birds and the other creatures at Riverside. Now, YOU have become a part of this love story!

I'm honored to introduce you to Frankie and Blossom…

Thank you and Blessings!

K.S. Wuertz

PUBLISHER'S NOTE: This book is a work of fiction based upon real events. All Names, places, characters and incidents either are a product of the author's imagination or are used fictionally, and any resemblance to actual persons: living or dead, to places, business establishments, towns and communities, or events is entirely coincidental.

To find other books (in this series or others) by K.S. Wuertz, order additional print or electronic copies of *Frankie and Blossom: A Honkin' Great Love Story* or to contact the author visit:

www.kswuertz.com

Cover Design and Illustrations by K. S. Wuertz, by staff/affiliates at Riverside Cemetery, Deb and Randy Hoyt, or are public domain.

First Edition: January 2024

Created and Published in the USA, Mimosa Lake Press

Library of Congress Cataloging- in- Publication Data

Wuertz, Kimberlee S.

Frankie Meets Blossom: A Honkin' Great Love Story/Kimberlee S. Wuertz – 1st Edition

ISBN: 9798873750160

Frankie and Blossom

If two souls are meant to be together – nothing on earth will keep them apart, no matter how unlikely it may seem. Destiny is sparked the moment they meet. Of course, they bring their life history to one another, stuffed in that invisible suitcase we all carry with us called - "experience".

Frankie and Blossom are just such a couple. Their unlikely love story grew from the depths of their loneliness. It began with some 'angel humans' who understood that love is meant for all – whether cat or canary, giraffe or goldfish, dog or dove, human or hyena, or even goose and gander.

Photo of the carving gifted to the Riverside Cemetery by Kim Hornberg

But, oh my!
I do get ahead of myself,
especially when I think about
love stories with happy endings.

When Frankie was born with blue eyes,
his fate was sealed as one of the most handsome
ganders on the planet!
Well, certainly in all of Iowa.

His name at birth was Hansel. Gretel was his partner. After he and Gretel moved to Randy and Deb Hoyt's Healing Hearts with Horses Animal Rescue Farm and Sanctuary, most people just called him "Handsome".

Of course, he was handsome, with those lovely blue eyes. Randy began calling him Frankie (after Frank Sinatra). Frankie and Randy spent their days hanging out together at the farm.

The rescue farm had many visitors. Frankie enjoyed "talking" to anyone who came to visit, as long as they didn't run from him.

(He did enjoy a good chase now and then.)

Frankie and Gretel had tried to have babies, but their eggs didn't hatch. Then Gretel laid three eggs in the front yard by the farmhouse at the sanctuary. Deb and Randy were concerned. There was no protection for Gretel as she sat on her nest.

But Gretel was faithful to her eggs. She stayed on the nest and kept them warm. Frankie checked on her and helped as he could, but you know how a mother is with her babies. Would one of the goslings have blue eyes, like Frankie? The whole farm waited for the impending hatching.

But one morning,
when Randy came out to check on Gretel,
his heart broke.
The eggs were broken. There was nothing left of Gretel
but some feathers strewn about the nesting area.
Frankie was nowhere to be found.

Everyone at the sanctuary was sad.

Later that day, their hearts were lifted when Frankie returned home.
Knowing his Gretel was gone, broke Frankie's heart.

You see, geese are very committed souls.

Frankie was lonely and sad. No one knew what to do.

Everyone gave him special attention. While he still loved talking to his humans, life just wasn't the same without Gretel.

Meanwhile, Blossom was living 70 miles away at Riverside Cemetery in Marshalltown, with her partner, Bud.

Bud and Blossom had great adventures together.

There was the time they crossed North Center Street to get to Riverview Park.

They were looking for a place to picnic. How were they to know they would become the Number One (and Two) most wanted geese in Marshall County, Iowa that day?

They were astonished when their humans from the cemetery came to drive them home. They weren't ready to return to their lake at the cemetery quite yet. So, they gave their humans a run for their money.

But loving humans can be persistent. Eventually Bud, then Blossom, were reluctantly captured and taken home before nightfall. Who knew their people would get in such a tizzy over a picnic and walk to the park?

After that, Bud and Blossom stuck a bit closer to home. In the evenings, they rested with the other resting human souls. Their days were spent eating, swimming and honking.

It was goose paradise.

Unfortunately, like Frankie, Blossom was suddenly widowed one night.

No one knows what happened to Bud. His lifeless body was found in the Catholic section of the cemetery. Like at the animal sanctuary, all the humans, birds, swans and other animals grieved.

Perhaps it was a fox, or maybe some other animal attacked Bud. No one really knows.

Bud was buried under a beautiful tree.

Blossom, was alone.

Oh, the swans were still there, and the ducks. Many people came to pay their respects and feed Blossom bread.

But Blossom took the loss of her beloved Bud very hard.

Blossom spent hours staring at her reflection in the cemetery office window.

She sought comfort by looking at "another" goose. But a reflection is far from the real thing.

The bleak, cold Iowa winter wasn't helping anyone feel better.

Blossom wandered around the lake
and the graves. Her humans were
very concerned.

Like with Frankie, there was
no consoling Blossom.

Valentine's Day was coming. That gave Blossom's human, Dorie an idea!

She would play cupid!

It was the perfect time to see if there were any ganders looking for a <u>very attractive,</u> widowed goose.

Dorie sprang into action. She turned to the internet!

She didn't know if there were any "*Goose meets Gander*" dating sites. But heck, there's everything else on the internet.

Dorie put Blossom's story on social media. She didn't know what would happen or what could happen. But Blossom needed help, so Dorie told the world about Blossom's plight:

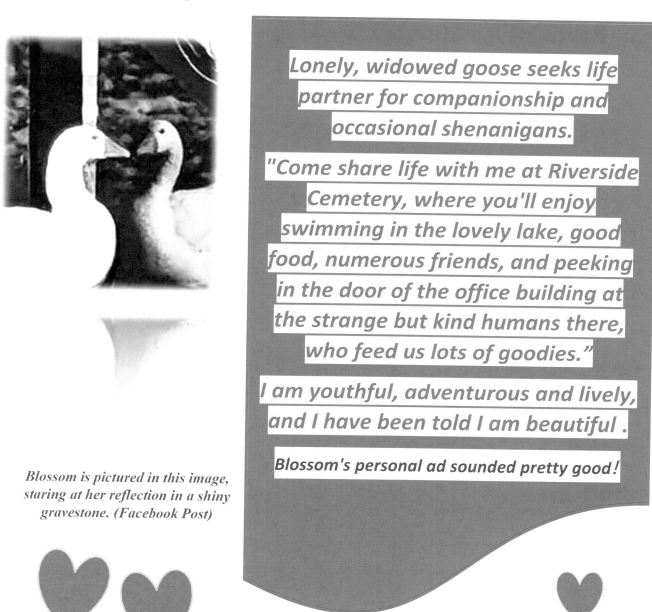

Blossom is pictured in this image, staring at her reflection in a shiny gravestone. (Facebook Post)

Lonely, widowed goose seeks life partner for companionship and occasional shenanigans.

"Come share life with me at Riverside Cemetery, where you'll enjoy swimming in the lovely lake, good food, numerous friends, and peeking in the door of the office building at the strange but kind humans there, who feed us lots of goodies."

I am youthful, adventurous and lively, and I have been told I am beautiful .

Blossom's personal ad sounded pretty good!

Then, Dorie held her breath.

Could Blossom find love again?

Is it too much to hope that true love can come twice to one lifetime?

But Valentine's Day was here, the time of year that brings hope to all lonely hearts.

After seeing Dorie's plea, Deb and Randy discussed Frankie's situation. It was especially hard on Randy.

"He's getting along fine. Yes, he's been lonely, but we're together all day." Randy said to Deb. Still, every evening they watched Frankie outside, alone.

"I want him to be happy." Randy's heart was heavy. After much thought, and because they loved Frankie so much, they contacted Dorie.

Dear Dorie and Blossom:

Our Frankie recently became a widower. Although it breaks our hearts, we want Frankie to heal his heart and be his happy self again.

Can we bring Frankie to meet Blossom? Frankie is known as one of Iowa's most handsome ganders, maybe Blossom will think so, too.

Deb and Randy Hoyt, and Frankie

Soon the day came for Frankie to leave the farm sanctuary for good. To say he was unhappy when Deb and Randy loaded him in the car was an understatement! He honked in protest during much of the long drive.

Upon arrival, Frankie immediately flew off for parts unknown. The hunt for Frankie was on! At dark, the hunt was called off for the night. Everyone was worried. No, not just worried – heartsick.

Deb and Randy didn't sleep a wink. Dorie, Mike and the other cemetery caregivers were reminded of Bud and Blossom's picnic trip to the park all those years ago. Had they made a mistake, bringing Frankie to Marshalltown?

The next morning, the hunt resumed. Blossom held vigil by the pond (*though she wasn't sure why or who she was waiting for*).

**That afternoon,
Frankie was found and returned as quickly as
he had gone.** *(With Caregiver Mike's help…)*

Blossom meets Frankie...with Mike's help.

For Blossom, it had been just another day...

Until, it wasn't!

She was used to cars coming and going. But when the door opened on Frankie's car, she opened her wings and ran toward him.
It was like she was coming home!

Frankie didn't know what to think. It was such a different place than the farm. Being so personable and handsome, he took a chance and went to Blossom. She couldn't wait to show him their beautiful lake.

There was a stop by the
bread box for a bite from
the humans. Then a nod to
Bud, whose grave rested
under a nearby tree.

Since then, they've had a
couple of little glitches, like
all new couples do. But it's
been a match made in
heaven - with the help of
the internet..

Little Free Breadbox
Leave a little, take a little
feed the birds!

Frankie and Blossom have been together ever since.

Deb and Randy, who loved
Frankie so much that they let him fly away
to Blossom, come by for "double dates"
whenever they can. Dorie, Mike and the
cemetery staff are always nearby.

**Sorrow, grief, loneliness, trials and tribulation
can come to any beating heart.
Whether it walks on 2, 4, 8, or even 1300 legs!
(*That's a millipede by the way,
because who am I to say that millipedes
don't grieve, love, or hope for love?*)**

Frankie and Blossom know it's true.

When love searches, it doesn't matter where we are.
Love will find us.
Even in Iowa.
Even in February.
Even in a cemetery.

So if you go to Marshalltown, Iowa,
come on by Riverside Cemetery for a visit.
Frankie is always ready to swap a honk or two.
Blossom will be right there, happily listening as
Frankie takes the lead.

Be sure to bring a snack. You'll probably be there longer than you expect. Corn is great, but bread is always on the menu, Especially when it's shared with love.

The End

To those who made this book possible... Thank You!

Randy and Deb Hoyt

Steve Hartman and Cameraman Bob (retired), CBS News

Steve Hartman and Dorie Tammen

Frankie and Blossom. Of Course!

Frankie and Mike, their Caregiver

...And the Riverside Cemetery staff who care for Frankie, Blossom and all the animals every day~

BOOKS BY K. S. WUERTZ

THE MIMOSA LAKE SERIES

Life at Mimosa Lake:

The Story of the Winter Visitor (Vol. 1 (2nd Edition))

The recession left River Ivery and her Mimosa Lake neighbors feeling isolated and hopeless. River knows something must change. But how? God's answer is the Winter Visitor. With loving presence, the Visitor offers renewal to the neighbors. But will they take it? Only the coming of spring will tell.

Life at Mimosa Lake:

Warm Days and Leda Clay (Vol. 2 (2nd Edition))

Thanks to the eagles that wintered at Mimosa Lake, the neighbors are looking forward to spring. But are they standing on Leda clay that's ready to slide away beneath their feet? Join River and all her Mimosa Lake neighbors, as they rely on their faith to give them sure footing through an ever-changing landscape. With God's help, they just might learn that falling down a slippery slope can land you in unexpected blessings.

Life at Mimosa Lake:
Spring Sprouts and Fall Ashes (Vol. 3)

The neighbors expect the unexpected at Mimosa Lake. They've come to rely on the eagles to fly in with the promise of better days on their wingtips. The eagles are nesting on Scout Point Island, but where are those better days? Join River, Dock, Georgia, Tim and all the neighbors, as they are tested in a firestorm of fear, grief, heat, lust and loss. But with God's help, and under the eagles' watchful eyes, the neighbors may discover the strongest spring sprouts grow from fall's ashes.

Life at Mimosa Lake:
The Shadows of Comfort (Vol. 4)

Who would burn down the Canopy? The accusation of arson against River Ivery has catapulted her into a spiritual desert. Dock Crayton knows his wife Trixie and River are innocent. But how can he prove it? Join the Mimosa Lake neighbors as they wait, search and walk through the sand and the shadows. Maybe comfort rests in the darkest of shadows. After all, darkness rests against the light. Doesn't it?

2nd Edition out in 2025

Life at Mimosa Lake:

Grapevines and Other Saving Graces (Vol. 5)

Could life be settling down at Mimosa Lake? The false accusations against River and Trixie have left their scars. Why is nothing the same? Catching Thad in the arms of his old love has something to do with it. What about Herbert, and Georgia, and the day Franklin finds Frances laying in her yard? At Mimosa, it can be an afternoon float on the Dogwood River or a trip over the cliffs at Scout Point Island. You just never know.

2nd Edition out in 2025

Life at Mimosa Lake:

The Worn Path by the Shore (Vol. 6)

Will River and Thad keep their wedding date? They have a discovery to make before they can meet at the altar. Loli's bravely battling her cancer, but Trixie can see she's tired. Georgia Lemonn says it's time to resign as MOB president. What! Franklin Sheldon's walking a rocky path these days, but like Tim Cole, he continues on, step by step. Come celebrate the joy of life turning, and the comfort of old familiar friends. Grab your walking stick, they're waiting for you at Mimosa Lake.

2nd Edition due in 2026

CHRISTMAS AT MIMOSA LAKE SERIES   NOVELLAS

Merry Christmas from Mimosa Lake!

Christmas at Mimosa Lake:

The Nativity (Vol 1)

In December 2011, Mimosa Lake is cluttered with unfulfilled wishes, burned out buildings, strange people and tempers flaring. What a season! River, Dock, Georgia, Franklin, Tim, and all the neighbors are searching for a place to rest. It isn't easy to find room at the Inn, especially when it's burned down. Sometimes, peace comes when we stand in the cold, at the edge of a manger. Walk with the neighbors as they seek shelter and find their joy in *The Nativity*.

Christmas at Mimosa Lake:

The Wise Men (Vol 2)

River is no longer lost in her own spiritual desert but she still doesn't have her bearings. Blessedly she has three wise men who know how to help her. Dock Crayton, forever the fixer, believes his Christmas surprise will fix his wife's pain. But he didn't count on falling in love while Christmas shopping. Still, the neighbors are loved: *Good tidings of great joy* await them, if they can follow their hearts.

Christmas at Mimosa Lake:
Angels on High (Vol 3)

River's travels lead her to the blessing of strangers, who take her in from the winter storm. Who are these kind folks? The Mimosa Lake Angel is busy this season. Alvin Owens is in the Canopy kitchen burning oil. Taylor Ivery's tractor lost its brakes going down the cliff road with a wagon filled with carolers. Angels abound! Will Herbert Potts notice? It's the season of joy and song. Rejoice! The spirit is with us!

Christmas at Mimosa Lake:
Shepherds Abiding (Vol 4)

Is it really as simple as having others to love? River and Thad are peacefully asleep in their dream home on the hill when life takes an unexpected turn. A winter twist befalls the Owens. Should Christmas be cancelled this year? The neighbors continue to help, pray, bring food, and decorate the Canopy, as the angels and eagles watch over them. It's a different holiday season at Mimosa Lake. Join the neighbors in this final tale from the shores of Mimosa Lake.

You can read these Christmas novellas as a part of the Mimosa Lake novel series or as stand-alones!

(Sometimes, we all need a good Christmas story.)

NOVELS

SOUL SEARCHING

What Happens When We Die?

Mercedes Beecher has it all. Money. Beauty. Fame. Fortune. Family. Her life looks great. But then, it's brutally cut short. Mercedes isn't ready to go. She has unfinished business. But she's not playing on her own terms any longer. And… where is she? So, her search begins.

But for what?

How many chances do we get?

THE MYSTERY OF MOON MOUNTAIN

Does anybody really know what happened on Moon Mountain?

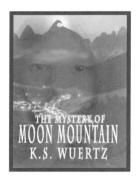

Tulip Burk Leahy was born under the light of the full moon as it rested in Moon Mountain. All the Burk women born this way are special: 'gifted seers'. They work to reconcile spirits of the living and dead.

Tulip keeps the secrets and lies of her neighbors and as just as many of her own. Now she may be forced to tell what ain't to be spoken of. Tulip only wants to live quietly in the shadow of Moon Mountain, but that's not her fate.

Must the truth be told?

Isn't it best to leave some things unspoken?

SHORT WORK

31 Days at Mimosa Lake:
Neighborly Devotionals from the Heart

Mimosa Lake has inspired the neighbors to reflect on some of their favorite Scripture passages. Like sunlight sparkling on the water, this book is filled with HOPE! Join all your favorite Mimosa neighbors, and the author, for some down-to-earth devotion to Heaven above! The good news awaits. Rejoice!

moving toward center

This fiction/non-fiction mix of short stories, essays, songs, poetry and devotionals, reveal my journey as a writer, daughter, friend, sufferer, lover, a believer – a human being. I believe you will see yourself in these pages."

moving toward center holds new work and some previously unpublished pieces in a page turner that offers a little mystery, encourages hope, may bring a tear to your eye and definitely a smile!

whispers of center

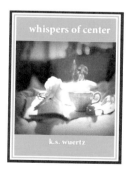

K.S. Wuertz opens her private notebook to share to share her reflections on our present times in thoughtful prose and poetry about Life, Loss and Love.

whispers of center will gently capture your heart and assure you that indeed, we all belong to something much greater than ourselves and each other. These words, will you leave you with an appreciation for the life journeys we all share.

THE SOULS AND PAWS SERIES

Love Stories for Everyone

A portion of the proceeds from this series go to support animal welfare.

Levi

The Wonderfully Spectacular, Incredibly Amazing

Angel Cat:

A Love Story for Everyone!

Levi shares a special love that fills heaven and earth. Join this big, orange cat, as he lives out his earthly days. But when he dies, he finds he can't leave the one he loves to grieve alone. Blessedly, the Top Cat gives him wings and the faith to mend broken hearts. Like every great love story, Levi's story ends happily ever after!

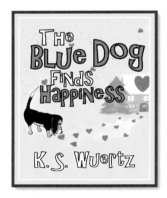

The Blue Dog Finds Happiness

Blue the beagle isn't sure where he's going, but it's a long way from Mama's. He's met a lot of people along the way – not all of them kind. Will he ever find happiness? Well, he can tell you!

<u>Love Stories for Everyone</u>

<u>A portion of the proceeds from this series go to support animal welfare.</u>

Katnapped! Pete Discovers Treasure

Pete's just an ordinary alley cat whose luck changed the day he moved in with 'his' two girls. His life was filled with walks, naps, parties and even a can of tuna once in a while. But one day, an evil stranger takes him away from it all. How can being katnapped help an alley cat discover hidden treasure? It's a story only Pete can tell!

Frankie and Blossom: A Honkin' Great Love Story

Blossom and Frankie led very separate lives, but suddenly, they shared something very personal. When each lost their spouse (geese mate for life you know), they were left lonely and grieving. Their "humans" turned to… where else? The internet! If these unlikely internet singles could be brought together, would it work? Sometimes reality is stranger (and better) than fiction… just ask Frankie and Blossom. *(Their answer might just warm your heart!)*

Lex: A Sheep in Wolf's Clothing

Coming

Fall 2025

FOR ADULTS AND CHILDREN

TO READ TOGETHER

It All Happened at the Old Oak Tree

At first glance, everything seems quiet at the Old Oak Tree, but take a closer look. Peek into the secret lives of some of creatures who come to: play, work, hide, jump, run, rest or just be near – the star of the forest – the place where it's all happening . . . the Old Oak Tree.

Buggin' the Birds

What's the world look like from a bug's eye view? The bugs watch everything around them, especially the birds. Butterfly, Moth, Ladybug, Spider, the Honeybees and so many other bugs are waiting to tell you secrets about their feathered friends.

K S WUERTZ

Is published in several anthologies, magazines, newspapers, devotionals, blogs and various publications devoted to spiritual and purposeful living.

Made in the USA
Columbia, SC
20 August 2024

40691720R00035